# Profitable New T Shirt Printing Business

CW00502699

Lee Lister is a Business Consultant with more than 25 year's consultancy experience for many household names. She is known as The Bid Manager or The Biz Guru.

From an early age she began an unparalleled journey through business consulting that continues to span across the UK, USA, Europe and Asia. She has consulted for many companies all over the world. Specialising in business change management, start up consultancy and trouble shooting. She is highly skilled in seminars, lectures and corporate presentations on business, project management and bid management. Lee's experience in marketing and internet marketing is also keenly sought after.

She is a prolific published writer of books, ebooks and articles on business, entrepreneurship and bid management. She can easily be found on major search engines and Amazon.

## Profitable New T Shirt Printing Business

Learn how to set up a profitable business, understand how to overcome the strains and stresses of a new company and become a Successful Entrepreneur.

**www.ProfitableNewBusiness.com**

**Author: Lee Lister**

First published in Great Britain in 2009.

*Part published as Start My New T Shirt Printing Business.*

**ISBN:** 978-0-9563861-5-1

**This book is dedicated to my daughter Kerry Lister for whom I have always strived to be my best.**

**Other books available include:**

Entrepreneur's Apprentice

How Much Does It Cost To Start A Business?

Start My New Party Selling Business

Start My New Cake Decorating Business

Profitable New Manicurist Business

Profitable New Quilting Business

Profitable New Bottled Water Business

## Contents

## Legal Notice

**W**e do not believe in get rich quick schemes. We do believe that business is equal parts of inspiration, hard work and luck. We ensure that every book that we sell will be interesting and useful to our clients. Every effort has been made to accurately represent our product and it's potential. Any testimonials and examples used are not intended to represent the average purchaser and are not intended to guarantee that anyone will achieve the same or similar results

**Please remember** that each individual's success depends on his or her background, dedication, desire, and motivation. As with any business endeavour, there is an inherent risk of loss of capital. **There is no guarantee that you will earn any money**. This book will provide you with a number of suggestions you can use to better guarantee your chances for success. **We do not and cannot guarantee any level of profits.**

This book is written with the warning that any and every business venture contains risks, and any number of alternatives. We do not suggest that any one way is the right way or that our suggestions are the only way. On the contrary, we advise that before investing any money in a business venture you seek counselling and help from a qualified accountant and/or attorney.

> **You read and use this book on the strict understanding that you alone are responsible for the success or failure of your business decisions relating to any information presented by our company Biz Guru Ltd.**

## Introduction

T shirt printing is a very inexpensive business to start and is in high demand although a very competitive area. T Shirt printing equipment is very low in cost. You can also buy shirts for T shirt printing at low wholesale prices, with good potential profit levels.

Personalisation is what makes custom T shirt printing so appealing. Custom T shirt printing is in higher demand then any other type of shirt printing and has several benefits including its uniqueness, company branding and team loyalty.

With custom T shirt printing you can personalise any shirt with any type of picture you want. It can be a simple message with a family photo or a favourite character with your name.

A large and growing business demand for T shirt printing is that of branding. Companies ask for a set of T shirts for their staff, all with the company branding on them and perhaps their name as well.

Similarly local sports teams will also issue T shirts or polo shirts for their members and followers. Lastly if you get big enough you may be able to print the T shirts for local schools or nurseries. Some other potential clients could include fraternities, churches, athletic teams, sororities and local youth clubs.

## What Kind Of T Shirt Business Do You Want To Run?

The T shirt printing business is very competitive so you need to have your own niche. Whether it is the selection of your shirts, your designs, your services or who you sell to you MUST find your niche quickly.

There are two key things you need to look at first of all. These are Subject Area and Target Audience.

## Subject Area and Theme

Some subjects and themes do better than others and if you decide to do too many of them then your business will look unfocussed and unstructured. So it is important to choose your subject area and theme very quickly. It also makes it so much easier to promote your business if you can say "Xeon for Fantasy T Shirts" for example.

Look at one key theme or subject area and then look at adding complimentary themes or subjects as you get asked or you wish to expand. Choosing a theme that particularly interests you is a good way to start. Some themes might be:

- Fantasy
- Groups and bands
- Sports
- Animals and pets

You might also look at your company specialising in the following kind of themes:

- Pets
- Family or children
- Digital photos
- Hen nights and stag nights
- Club
- Sport
- Uniforms

## Target Audience

Now you need to decide who you are targeting. That is what age group, income level and geographic area.  This will help you with your marketing so that you do not market or advertise where your potential buyers are not situated.

Of course your themes and designs will need to be compatible with your target audience.

## Research

Now you will need to undertake your research. You will need to be able to find enough designs to ensure that you have enough of them for a good, attractive and varied range.
You will also need to undertake similar research to ensure that you can also find the appropriate T shirts, fleeces etc.

If you want your T shirts to be topical, you might also like to keep an eye on the news and different trends.

## Ways To Print Your T shirts

There are a number of ways to print T shirts, here are the most common.

## Heat Transfer Equipment

The first of these T shirt printing machines are what are known as heat transfer machines. Heat transfer machines are very popular and for good reason as they are one of the most affordable types of T shirt printing machines that you can find on the market. They are good for the environment and give the creator of the shirts more flexibility and control as well as providing ease of transferring the design onto the shirt. You can use them for small orders, while still having the production at a reasonable cost. Heat transfer machines are also portable and, as small in size, they can be taken just about anywhere such as a market stall.

There are two types of machines, drum and press. The clam type press machine is the best choice for a beginner or if you are expecting to produce small runs of T shirts.

It looks like a slightly larger toasted sandwich machine and it will be easy to store in your own home or garage. The larger press machines are called Swing Presses and give you greater speed and accuracy but take up a lot more space. Drum machines are not so often used, but give you the option to print larger items such as posters.

There is a cheaper version of heat transfer, in that you can also print directly onto special paper and then iron the paper onto your T shirt.

It is possible to buy a large range of transfers suitable for ironing or heat pressing onto T shirts and other items from the internet.

You might also buy T shirt printing software to produce your designs. The software comes with numerous fonts and some stock images; some even come with paper and a free T shirt. Read about all of them so you can decide which would be better for you. The prices ranges will vary so if you want high quality software with lots of options, plan to spend more. Sometimes the money is worth the end result.

When searching for your preferred equipment, you will be offered lots of kits that provide you with the printing machine, software, transfers etc. Often these save you money.

## Heat Transfer Printing

You can obtain your design either by printing off your won design onto special heat transfer paper or by buying one the of numerous available transfers.

When setting up your design, you need to make sure your image is 'mirrored.' This way it will not be reversed when you apply it to your T shirt.

Have your image ready on your computer to print. Check to make sure you have correctly loaded paper into the printer before you print.

If you are using an iron, it needs to be hot with no steam or moisture. That could affect the smoothness of the image. You need to see what the instructions say about of how long to leave the iron on. The fabric of your T shirt may also have an effect on this.

The easiest T shirts to start on are white. If you use other colour fabrics, you need to check first that the T shirt colour does not merge with your design when it is heat transferred.

## Ink Jet Printing

Inkjet machines print the object directly onto the shirt unlike the multiple steps to and/or intense heat used in the other methods. Inkjet machines also have a very fast turnaround time for producing shirts. This is an added bonus for anyone who needs quick production times to meet their businesses T shirt printing needs. Most inkjet machines can use any type of graphics program and can also print on many different types of shirts that range form one-hundred percent cotton shirts all the way to fifty-fifty shirts.

Like heat transfer machines, inkjet machines are mobile and can be taken anywhere. You will be restricted by the ability to get the garment into the printer – so fleeces and caps will probably not be possible. As your budget increases it is possible to buy specialist printers that will print onto several T shirts, fleeces or even caps.

## Screen Printing

Screen printing is one of the early methods of printing. It involves the passing of ink or any other printing medium through a mesh or 'screen' that has been stretched on a frame, and to which a stencil has been applied. The stencil openings determine the image that will thus be imprinted.

You first of all make up your design using Adobe Illustrator or Freehand and then save as a vector art work.

Make up you screens using a mesh surface. The screen should look like a negative of your design. The areas that are *not* to be printed are masked out on the screen.

The screen is then positioned over the item and a dollop of ink placed on the frame. A squeegee is then run over the screen so that the first colour is printed on the T shirt. The T shirt is then placed under a heat source until it is dried. The activity is repeated for each colour.

## Selling Via Web Sites

You can also find several web sites such as café press where you can upload your own designs and have them printed onto T shirts for you. Whilst this may seem tempting, it is a very expensive way to do things and if you can do it – why can't your customers? Also remember that you will make little profit as you will also have to pay for the T shirt to be printed, sent to you and packed in the web sites package – so you will also need to repackage it as well.

## Embroidery

Something a little different that you might think of to enhance your offerings is the opportunity to embroider names and wordings onto a new T shirt. It is possible to buy such machines that you can programme to embroider onto T shirts and caps.

## Digital Photos

With the rise of good digital cameras it is possible to capture some great pictures, print them off on heat transfer paper and then transfer them to a T shirt. Remembering to invert your image of course.

How about setting up a market stall, taking photos of children or pets and then transferring them onto a T shirt?

If you become a proficient photographer then there are some great photos you can take.

## Getting Your Business Started

This is a business that you can run quite easily from home with just a telephone and a simple filing system.

Most countries and states require some kind of licensing and registration so you should check this out. It would also be advisable to have a background check if this is available. You should also obtain the appropriate insurance. It would also be good to have at least two checkable references. Once you have all of these you should take photocopies of these and put them together as a Sales Pack.

## Your Brochure

Your brochure can be quickly made up on a PC. Design a one page description of your business and the kind of work that you do. Include your contact details and company name. Do not include too many words – just make it catchy, memorable and informative. You can include a couple of graphics which you can easily find on the internet.

If you wish you can also include a business card. These can be professionally produced from web sites such as vistaprint or from you local stationary store or printer.

## Uniform

It would be a good idea to give yourself some kind of uniform such are one of your T shirts or sweaters printed with your company name and one of your great designs.

Match your colours of your uniform and your equipment to your company colours. This makes you look like a professional company. Make sure that everything is cleaned regularly – including your equipment.

## Your Sales Pack

Your Sales Pack is the major step in your T shirt business – it is what makes your business professional and moves you to the next level. It allows you to work with larger companies or clubs who want to buy your goods in bigger volumes.

The Sales Pack must contain a printout or photocopy of your terms and conditions, insurance and background check, references and your brochure.

In your terms and conditions you should explain the details of your working policy. This will give information such as: your hours of operation; when a deposit and full payment is due; if you will deliver or not etc.

All these details should be included in your terms and conditions in order to not only look organised and professional but also to avoid misunderstandings in the future.

## Your Equipment

The core of your T shirt printing business will be your choice of printing methods and the quality of shirts and inks.

There are a considerable number of kits for sale on the internet and you should investigate the contents, quality and cost of them quite thoroughly before making your choice. A good iron is also a good idea to place your heat transfer paper on the T shirt if you are using this method, but mostly to ensure that the finished T shirt looks its best.

Once you have decided whether you are printing only T shirts or a mixture of T shirts, polo shirts, fleeces, caps etc. you will need to ensure that you keep a good inventory of supplies in various designs as well as keep changing your designs. When choosing your shirt, you want to be sure it is clean and wrinkle free so that the design comes out clean and smooth with no lines or dirty smudges. Cotton and poly/cotton blend are the best materials to use for this, but you can use whatever fabric you choose.

The better quality your products and more unique your designs, the more customers will keep returning and recommending your services to others.

To produce and set up your designs you will need a good PC and colour printer. It is possible now to get a good colour laser printer at a reasonable price which will give you a good quality design.

It would greatly help your business to obtain good design software in order to manipulate your designs and print them off directly to your T shirt or the heat transfer paper.

You are also able to buy heat transfer paper with designs already printed on them and it would be a good idea to have a collection of these to ensue that you have a selection of designs to start your business off.

You will also need a supply of good labels so that you can stitch your own brand into the shirts and of course some packaging in which to wrap your finished product.

This should be cellophane for the T shirt and boxes for mailing. You might also supply carrier bags at point of sale. You should include a brochure or business card/postcard in each package you send off. Your cellophane packaging that you pack your T shirt in should have your company name and contact details on.

You might also consider a message board in your office to hold both messages and design ideas you have found. Lastly you will need an accountancy package or MsExcel to keep your accounts and MsWord for your invoices/receipts and correspondence. Email will make your customer correspondence quicker and easier for both you and your customers.

## Equipment List

| Equipment List | √ |
|---|---|
| PC | |
| Design Software | |
| Colour Printer – laser or inkjet | |
| Press or similar | |
| Transfer Paper | |
| CD/DVD's of designs | |
| Paper for invoices, receipts, correspondence, marketing etc. | |
| Sales Pack | |
| White T shirts | |
| Coloured T shirts | |
| Branded labels | |
| Iron | |
| Packaging, cellophane, boxes, bags | |
| Sales Pack | |
| Business Cards | |
| Brochures and flyers | |
| Message board | |
| Accountancy package | |
| MsOffice | |
| Email account | |

### Finding Your Designs

Some people think that making a T shirt printing design is complicated and a hard task. This is false. Making a T shirt printing design is one of the simplest things that you can do. In fact, you do not need to be an artist or even artistic to make a great T shirt printing design.

Creating a design for T shirt printing is simple because it can be anything. Many popular designs, especially for children, can be simple outlines and even stick figures that have funny phrases or slogans on them.

The first part of making your design is to know what you want to make. Are you aiming to make a design that will be funny? Or are you looking for an eye catching design? Your design can range from anything to everything. The most important part of making a design is to know what message and affect it will have from all that see it.

Now that you know what type of message or feeling you want your design to present, you are ready to start designing. If you are not the greatest artist or have problems thinking up a design, there are some places that you can find ideas from. Going to such places as your local library or even book store are some great places to find designs. Even looking through a magazine or looking at ads can help you generate ideas to create some designs.

There are many great drawings made for children that are designed by children. Simple drawings that your kids can make, whether they are stick figures or more complex drawings can become a great design pattern.

On the internet you can find many clip art and stock photograph sites that allow you to buy pictures providing that you include their copyright somewhere. Just read the terms and conditions very carefully.

Contact your local school or college and ask them if they want to contribute a design in exchange for a T shirt!

T shirt printing designs do not even have to be pictures. Producing a funny phrase in a colourful and fun text can be a great design. Producing a slogan or tag line with a simple pre-made logo can be another great way to create a simple design. There are many popular designs that are simple phrases or text with no pictures. Do not be afraid to make a word only design as this could be more successful then trying to create a picture. Just make it stand out and attractive.

Periodically tie-dye comes into fashion which can be another option.

Once you finish your design you can upload it to your computer and make it ready to imprint on a shirt.

## Looking At Funny T shirt Printings

Funny T shirt printing can be found anywhere and everywhere. It is true that funny T shirt printings are in very high demand and that they are sought after by not only younger people, but surprisingly, also older people. Yes, even the older people like to poke fun at things, whether it is their own limitations or even their own political views. When you go to such places as the San Francisco airport, you should not be surprised to find a shirt that says "The Governator," with a picture of the half man half machine terminator on his bike. No matter what the design or what is being made fun of, it only contributes to the humour that funny T shirt printings bring. Everyone wants to display these funny things which can certainly lighten up any person's day and really does bring attention to you.

Funny T shirt printings really are humorous. Despite some being offensive, they really do make you laugh, which is the point of them.

It is not surprising when you see funny T shirt printings for kids with such sayings as, "It's not my fault my brother did it!" and "I may be small, but don't let that fool ya, cause I am still the boss."

Shirts like these that are for children have proven to be irresistible for parents and have also have proven to be hot sellers.

The entire concept of funny T shirt printings is to bring humour. With funny T shirt printings, you can express a humorous statement or just poke fun at someone or something. Funny T shirt printings help people express themselves in a humorous way that usually always results in getting some sort of attention, as well as getting a few laughs at it.

Funny T shirt printings were made to bring out the fun side in people and to allow us to be not so conservative. Funny T shirt printings are really made for the open minded and those with a sense of humour, as they can offend someone who is not so light hearted.

There are many funny T shirt printings that are catered primarily towards adults and for good reason. Funny T shirt printings give adults many benefits. One of the biggest benefits of funny T shirt printings is that they allow us to be funny, goofy and yet still stay an adult at the same time.

It never hurts to get out and let loose every once in a while. So when you are feeling under the weather or having a stressed time, go find a funny T shirt printing. They are sure to brighten your day as well as anyone else who sees you wearing it.

## Pricing Your Services

Pricing is so important to the success of your business. You are in a very competitive business and you will be judged on your prices compared with your competitors. That said, T shirts are also somewhat an impulse buy so if you price them to meet this need, you are at an advantage.

When pricing your T shirt, fleece etc. look at the following costs:

- Buying your garment, including delivery costs or the cost of picking them up.
- You consumables such as heat transfers, dyes, print ink, paper etc.
- Designs, licences etc.
- A percentage of your equipment such as printers, computer, software etc.

You should set some money aside to build up your brand image by advertising and training any staff or distributors. People are more likely to buy if they know the product and how great they are.

## Will I Succeed?

You've got a great idea, you are pretty sure that what you have will sell; you've even got some cash together. Have you got what it will take to succeed? What else do you need?

**Vision:** You must be able to see where you are going and what the future will hold. See what others are not able to see and build your business on these visions.

**Courage:** The ability to act upon your vision despite having doubts. Having the courage to give up job security and a planned future for the opportunity of a successful new business.

**Strategy:** Having the courage to act upon your vision, you now need to build your strategies. You will need a business and a marketing strategy. These are the formulas that you will use to drive forward and manage your business.

**Planning Skills:** To ensure that you reach your vision, you need copious amounts of planning. Planning how you will reach your targets, how you will meet new changes and challenges and how you will improve your business. You will need a business plan and a marketing plan.

**Researching:** Having decided what your business is going to be, then you will need to find out who will want to buy from your business and at what price. This takes a fair amount of researching.

**Conceptualising:** Knowing what you want to sell and to whom, you now need to define your products and services. Brainstorm different things that you associate with your company. Include everything, good and bad, until you are out of ideas. Keep in mind that ideas generate ideas. Write everything down, this is how you move your company forward. Use this period to design your products, what you want your company to look like and how you want it to be perceived by your customers.

**Creativity:** You will need the ability to think outside of the box. Keep ahead of your competitors by coming up with new, unusual and unique concepts and solutions to their needs. You will need to create marketing materials, packaging and sales pitches – all will need verbal and visual creativity.

**Determination:** Along the way you will come across many hurdles and set backs, you will need to dig deep, make your changes and keep going. Determination and the belief in your visions and plans will keep you on the road to success.

**Humour:** When all the world seems against you and all seems to be going wrong, when your customers seem to be your worst enemy then you need a sense of humour to carry you forward.

Lastly you need good luck!

## A Successful Business Start up

Right you have sorted out your business ideas, you are ready to go ahead and you know what you want to sell and to whom. Now you need your business structure. These are all the things that make up your business. They include:

- **Legal Base:** This includes such factors as your licenses, insurances and setting up your company.

- **Your Market:** You need to decide who you want to market your services to and where they will be.

- **Your Services:** You now need to decide what services you are going to offer to these people, how you would like to package them and what prices you wish to charge.

- **Your Business Plan:** Whether you are looking for funding or not – a business plan is the foundation of a new business.

- **Your Funding:** You should now take your business plan and look around for funding, starting with your Bank.

- **Your Premises:** Look around for your new premises, preferably in the middle of your potential market. Remember that central to your success is the position you choose for your business. Foot traffic past your door and many potential customers within a short journey from your new business is vital to you finding customers.

- **Web Site:** Most businesses have them now – so even if you don't want to set one up now – at least buy and hold onto your domain name – in case someone else gets hold of it.

- **Your Staff:** Good staff that reflect your business ideals are vital so spend some time spend some time finding the best staff you can.

- **Marketing:** So important and so difficult to get right. Start with a good marketing strategy and go from there.

- **Grand Opening:** Make sure you make a splash and attract as much curiosity as possible.

## Your Business Framework

When starting a business of what ever kind, large or small, there is a always a require framework or scaffolding that you have to set up. Not only does this make your business much more effective, but it also saves you from a lot of embarrassing and costly problems. When you start up your business, remember to tick off the 10 items below and you will have a very sound start to your business. Here is your framework:

- **Business Name.** Choose an appropriate name that sums up what your business stands for. It has to be unique – try and ensure that a suitable domain name is also available as you will probably want a web site as well. The owner of an established web site might cause problems if you give your brick based business the same name – so be careful in your choice.

- **Your Business Entity.** Obtain professional advice as whether to the best way to set up your business as a limited company, partnership etc. Then register your company.

- **Patents and** Trademarks. If you have unique products then you need to ensure that you have registered your patents before your start trading. Similarly any product names, mottos, selling tags etc should be trademarked. Take professional advice on how to do this.

- **Licenses and Permits.** Ensure that you have all the licenses and permits that you are legally required to have.

- **Insurance.** You may think that you don't need this but you do and will. So take out property, business, vehicle liability, staff and disaster insurance. A good broker can advise you.

- **Taxes.** A necessary evil I am afraid. Register with your local tax collector. Set up a good accounting system and hire a good accountant.

- **Employment Laws.** Establish what you local employment laws are and ensure that you adhere to them. Set up employee guidelines and handbooks. Make sure you hire and fire legally.

- **Banking.** Visit your local banks and find the best business bank account and credit card for you business. Always keep your business and personal spending separate.

- **Business Plan.** This is your carefully written plan on how you want your company to operate, what you want to sell, where and to whom. It includes your business and marketing strategy as well as your financial standing and projections. This is the foundation of your business.

- **Liquid Cash.** Ensure that you have enough money to carry your through the first few months of your business as well as any foreseeable troublesome times ahead.

## The Nasties

Tax, Insurance and Licences these are the nasties of your business and all of them are compulsory! Look up your local state/county/country web site to see what licences you will need. Similarly your country's tax web site will tell you what taxes you will need to pay, how you register to pay them and what forms you will need to fill in to become legal. Don't attempt to work without them – there goes the way to a world of misery. Tax officials in particular, are trained to find and collect unpaid taxes and these are always combined with extra costs and penalties.

Operating your business in some countries will require you and your staff to be licensed before you can start work. This should be displayed on your premises or available for view by your customers.

You may also need a sales tax permit (USA and other sales tax based countries) or VAT registration (UK and some Europe and Asia) if you reach the VAT registration limit.

### Check List For Starting A New Business

You are ready to give up your job to start your new business, or even scarier, sink your savings into your new business. You just want to make sure that you have done everything possible to succeed, here is a check list for you.

1. Legal Stuff:

   • Do you have a memorable business name and the associated domain name?

   • Do you have a legal name and business entity?

   • Have you got all your licences?

   • Have you got all you certificates such as health and fire?

   • Have you registered everything you need to?

   • Have you told the tax department and got your numbers and details?

   • Are all your shares, statutory meetings etc correct?

   • Do you have all the patents and trademarks you need?

- Do you have the legal documents on your premises – leases, sales, mortgages etc.?
- Do you have all the posters and legal manuals etc that you need?

2. Strategies and Planning:
   - Do you have your Business Plan written?
   - Do you have a Business Strategy?
   - Do you have a Marketing Strategy?
   - Have you decided upon what Business Model you will use?

3. Protection:
   - Do you have your insurances for you, the company, liabilities, staff, premises and vehicles?
   - Have you got health insurance for you and staff if necessary?
   - Do you have your pension set up?

4. Finances:
   - Are your finances in place and have you signed all the forms necessary?
   - Do you have enough and on the right terms?

- Have you got your bank set up?
- Do you have your credit/debit card and payment processor set up?

5. Premises:

- Are your premises/office ready and equipped?
- Are all the utilities that you need connected – gas, electric, phone, broadband etc.?
- Do you have all the vehicles, computers and machinery that you need?

6. Staff:

- Do you have all the staff you need?
- Are they trained or ready to be trained?
- Do you have the necessary uniforms?

7. Marketing and Products:

- Have you checked who your potential market is and where these customers are hiding?
- Have you ensured that what you are selling is really, really what your proposed customers want?

- Do you have your pricing and upgrading sorted out?
- Do you have your branding sorted out?
- Do you have your starting marketing materials?
- Do you have standard replies to customer enquiries, invoices, receipts, business cards and letter heads sorted out?

## How Much Does It Cost To Start A Business?

You've got your business idea, think that you will be able to get a good loan and even have your business plan being written but.... The one big burning issue is – How much does it cost to start a business?

Well you first of all have to be realistic and understand that you are unlikely to make a profit within the first six months of business – so you should also budget for your first six months running costs. So here is your shopping list:

1)    **Purchase    or    rental    of lease/franchise/premises.**    This will include any Realtor fees, deposits and other legal expenses. Even small businesses need some kind of premises. To start with you can use a home office, but you are going to need somewhere to hold all that stock and materials that you will soon need as you get bigger. If you intend to only rent somewhere then take into account any deposit you will need as well as at least six month's rental costs.

2) **Cost of fit out and purchase of new equipment.** This will include any work that needs to be done on your premises as well as any equipment you have to buy in order to start and run your business. Often you can lease equipment in order to mitigate high start up costs. This also includes a car or van to deliver your stock to your distributors.

3) **Six months worth of advertising and marketing**. This will be particularly high at the start as you establish your business. Factor in some cold calling as well as a launch party or opening day. Marketing will include a lot of local advertising in order to attract good distributors.

4) **Legal, licensing and banking costs.** Your business will need to be set up correctly, licensed and have a good bank account. Sadly all of these require money. You may also need a payment processing service to use credit cards.

5) **Staff costs for six months.** Staff will be the basis of providing good service to your new customers. Make sure that you have enough money put aside to find them, train them and keep them! Much of your staff costs will be on a commission basis but you will still require admin staff and one or two "on staff" distributors and maybe warehouse staff as well. They will all want to be paid, often before you get paid for your sales.

6) **Uniforms, office and marketing supplies, packaging etc**. You will need to establish your brand. This means that your staff will need uniforms or at the least business cards and name tags. You will need brochures, adverts etc. If appropriate you will also need standardised packaging and documentation.

Your office will also need office equipment and supplies. You should also budget for designing your logo, brochures and adverts if you cannot do this yourself.

7) **Stock and supplies** – to keep you going for six months. This is a big expense because if you have 10 hosts they all need a core stock from which to sell from.

8) **Maintenance** for six months – your equipment will also need to keep going for six months. This includes your cars, computers, printers, copiers etc. Budget for a lot of printing ink!

9) **Any loans** that you have will also have to be paid. Again look at least at six months or until you break even and can pay the loan.

10) **Your salary** for six months – lastly you will need to pay your own bills and maintain your family during this time. You should expect that for a short while your standard of living will go down.

Add this up and add 10% for contingency and some good luck.

## Check List – Business Start Up Costs

| | |
|---|---|
| Purchase/Rental of lease/franchise/premises | √ |
| Realtor /Agent Fees | |
| Legal Fees | |
| Bank Fees | |
| Payment Processing Fees | |
| Business Consultancy Fees | |
| Business Planning Fees | |
| Deposits | |
| Business Equipment | |
| Manufacturing Equipment | |
| Office Equipment –fax, computer etc. | |
| Stock | |
| Office Stock – stationary, etc. | |
| Vehicle Detailing or sign writing | |
| Property Sign Writing | |
| Electric/Gas/Water/Phones | |
| Telecoms and internet | |
| Maintenance, Leasing and Hiring Fees | |
| Advertising and Marketing Costs | |
| Marketing Brochures, Business Cards etc. | |
| Design Costs | |
| Staff Costs | |
| Staff Uniforms | |
| Training | |
| Salary Costs | |

## Getting Started With Little Money

The age old question, you want to start your business but have little capital available. So how do you do it?

First of all have a look round for sources of borrowing money. The first obvious step is your bank. They are unlikely to lend money unless you have at least a deposit of 20%. Similarly if you approach the Small Business Bureau (USA) or Small Business Association (UK) or similar and ask for a guaranteed loan – they are probably going to want a similar deposit.

They may be able to offer you some advice as to where to go for funding. Your best bet is to get together a realistic business plan with what you wish to do and what it will cost in quite detailed format. Also include details of whom you expect your market to be and how large this market is.

A venture capitalist or angel investor is pretty much out of the question unless you have a really unique protected product or a very well established business.

Another source of business funding help may be to apply for a grant. They are difficult to get and you will have to have, not only a good case but a very well defined business idea.

So if you are capital poor the best advice is to start small. Look at a smaller version of what you intend to start up. Start with offering your services to local businesses first and working from a home office. Start selling from a mall kart or stall in a flea market, boot sale or local market place. You can also try eBay, CraigsList etc.

Start small and you have not risked too much. Build your business, establish your business name and build up capital and customers.

## What Goes Into A Business Plan?

You are ready to write your business plan for funding purposes, or you are starting a new business and know that you need one. So what goes into your business plan?

Well first of all, a good, well structured business plan can be the foundation to your new company. It is important that you spend some time ensuring that it is accurate. Here are the relative portions of your business plan.

- **Executive Summary**. This will be the first thing read by your potential investor and a strong executive summary with an overview of all that is required will ensure that the rest of your business plan is read.
- **Business Overview** and structure including shares issued and who owns them. This is where you describe your physical business, your business model, your Mission Statement, objectives of the business and key milestones,

• **Business Strategies** including business, financial, marketing and exit strategy. This is an important part of your business plan and details how you are going to mange your future business. The business strategy is how you run your business and how you intend to expand and grow from a new business. The financial strategy is how you will manage your finances, when you will invest, how much will go into research, if you will lease or buy etc. Your marketing strategy deals with marketing and advertising your business, to whom, how and at what costs. Your exit strategy is how the investor will be able to recoup their investment.

• **Markets**, which is who you expect to buy your products and services with some predictions of volumes.

• **Products**, which are the services and goods offered. You should include how they are manufactured or sourced as well as the fulfilment process.

• **Financials** such as costs, overheads, profit etc with realistic indications of why, how and when. You should also include your marketing and staffing budgets as well as overhead costs and your break even position.

• **Staffing** including resumes/CV's of major staff, brief terms of reference and an organisation chart.

• **The Way Forward**, what will happen in the future and how an investor will get their money back.

If you include all of these you will have a great business plan. This can seem daunting, which is why it can be worthwhile to employ a business planning consultant, who can also provide business consultancy. Good luck.

## Meeting The Bank Manager

**M**eeting with your bank to ask for a loan for your business is always going to be a challenge even if you have a profitable business. Here are a few ideas for you.

It's important to remember that your loan manager is probably a kind human being who has to adhere to the bank's rules on lending. The basic ones are:

- That you can repay the loan.
- The loan is business based and for a reasonable reason.
- That your business is viable and bona fida business.

Go to the meeting armed with:

- Your business details such as licenses etc.
- An outline of your business and how you see it expanding in the next few years.
- If you are seeking a large amount of money or have a new business then you must have a business plan.

- How much money you require and when you need it.
- How you will spend it and on what items.
- How your business will benefit, expand or profit from the loan.
- What collateral you can offer the bank – don't offer this until asked.
- When and how you will repay the loan.

Try not to hide anything – evasion is not a good reflection on your business acumen. If you are asked a difficult question then answer it as honestly as you can – but by putting a good spin so that you sound positive.

**Common Business Mistakes.**

All entrepreneurs have to learn from their own mistakes as they build their business, but wouldn't it be great to have some one tell you what the common mistakes are and how to avoid them? You Want a Successful Business – So Don't Do This!

- **Believing that you will start earning straight away**. All businesses take time to establish themselves – even internet based ones. People need to know where you are, what you sell and most importantly, that they can trust your company to deliver what it promises. Expect to spend at least 6 months working away at your business before you break even – sometimes longer.

- **Believing that you can set up a business and it continually earns for you.** Even a very profitable business needs continual management to ensure that your profit does not erode. Your products and marketing need to continually change to meet the changing circumstances in the real world.

- **Believing in Get Rich Quick Schemes:** A good business is established by part inspiration, part perspiration and just a little bit of luck!

- **Believing that you can earn whilst you are aware from the office.** Even if you fully automate your business and hire really good staff, there is always an element of "while the cat is away". That is why there are so many "absent owner" sales.

- **Being a single product company.** As good as your product may be, markets and tastes will change and so must you. If your product is very good – other companies will quickly take action to seize your market share by bringing in similar products at cheaper prices.

- **Not offering upgrades and enhancements.** It is far easier and cheaper to sell to existing customers. You do this by offering upgrades and enhancements to their existing products. You should have a group of products at several increasing price points.

- **Relaxing after you success.** Businesses need continual effort, management and improvements. Although a product launch is hard work, you should start on your next product shortly afterwards. This will give you sustainable success and several income streams.

- **Believing that a business can be established with little capital.** Marketing, infrastructure purchases, stock, advertising and staff all cost money and must be purchased in order to make a profit. Cash flow kills more business than anything else.

- **Believing that you know all you have to**. Your competitors may have been in the business longer than you have, your customers may be very knowledgeable. Meeting customer needs is a constantly changing landscape and you need to keep up to date on the latest trends and technology. You need to be able to project yourself as an expert in the field you work in. If you do not have this knowledge then learn it or buy it in!

- **Not investing in your staff.** Your staff are the public face of your business. They should be well trained, knowledgeable and well dressed as well as fully motivated to sell on your behalf.

- **Not motivating** your staff. Good staff are hard to find and difficult to keep. They help your business expand and be profitable. They will grow your business exponentially as word of mouth spreads.

- **Branding.** It is important that your company is recognised and has a good image. This helps spread the word about your services! Otherwise why would your customers hire you? Spend on your brand, its worth it!

Learn these lessons well, avoid the mistakes at all costs you should save valuable time and resources by doing things right the first time.

## Your Unique Selling Point

You've heard about a Unique Selling Point and guess that you want one but you have no idea what it is and why you need one. Often called the U.S.P – it means – "What makes your company, product and services different from all the other companies selling the same thing?

Now obviously in a crowded business environment – be it click or brick – you want your company to not only stand out but be memorable. You USP will do this for you.

## So how do I define my USP?

Have a look at you company and a few companies that you believe compete with you. Also look at a couple of companies who are trading as you would wish to trade in the next few years. For products we mean products, goods or services.

So, what product features could you have that would make you different from your competitors?

- Look at what products you sell the most often or most of.
- How do these products differ from each other?
- What benefits do these products provide?
- What better features do you/ you could provide?
- What features do competitor's products have that yours do not?
- What features do your products have that are different you're your competitors?

Make yourself stand out from your competitors and emphasise this in all your fully branded marketing materials and you should not only stand out from others but also look larger, more professional and memorable.

## Branding, The How's, What's And Why's

Your business brand says a lot about you and your business. If you create a strong brand image, it will elevate you above your peers and provide a good model for your product and service development as well as a sound foundation from which to expand your business.

## What is Branding?

Many people think that having a logo and maybe a short description of their services is all they need to set up their brand.  This is not so.

Your brand encompasses all that your business does, from first contact with your potential customers through to how your products are defined and sold.  Your brand is what defines and describes your business.  Look at any two different companies that compete in the same market and look at how people recognise and remember them.

For example look at Rolls Royce and Toyota - they both sell cars but each company is known for a different reason. Someone looking for a car on a budget would not go to Rolls Royce - yet both sell their cars on reliability. Clearly more people would aspire to purchase a Rolls Royce, but many also be happy to purchase a Toyota.

Look again at the perceived value of a brand. Why is the iPod the desired MP3 product when other brands have similar properties and reliabilities? People perceive the ipod to be superior and are willing to pay more for the pleasure of owning one. Indeed many people would not consider any other purchase. This is clever branding by Apple who marketed their product as being very desirable to certain markets.

## I Don't Have that Kind of Money - So Why do I Need to Create my Own Brand?

The main reason has to be to differentiate yourself. You are starting a business in a very crowded market so you need to stand out from the hobby workers and other competitors.

Branding also makes the promotion of your company and development of your products so much easier. There are thousands of new businesses and many times more web sites. You need to:

- Set yourself apart from the competition
- Make yourself memorable so that people will either look for your business or choose you above your competitors.
- When introducing your business to a new customer, your brand should go before you and communicate much of what you want to say.

Your T shirts will be easier to define and design, if you centre them around your brand definition. For example if you are selling fantasy T shirts your brand image will be totally different than if you are selling children's T shirts. You need to appeal to a different market – i.e. young adults as opposed to young children and their parents.

## So How Do I Create My Own Brand Then?

You brand must say:
- Who you are.
- What you do.
- How you do it.
- What the benefits of using your business are.

You brand MUST establish your company and build your credibility with your prospective customers.

In order to be able to do this you must first be able to describe what you want your business and products say, so start with your Mission Statement or Elevator Statement.

- **The Mission Statement** - this is what you want your business to be or do as it operates. You need to be realistic and focused. Being profitable is not a mission statement, but deciding what you want to do to be profitable is.

- **The Elevator Statement** - This is 1-4 sentences that you would use to describe your business, in the time that it takes to travel in an elevator - or a few minutes. It is used when meeting new people who ask "and what do you do?" or as an introduction when networking.

## What Should Be Described Within My Brand?

First of all, pretend that you are one of your target customers and list 5 things that they will be seeking from your product. These items would encompass a short definition of one of more of the following:

- Price.
- Quality.
- Service.
- Support.
- Scarcity or availability.
- How and when delivered.
- Accessibility.
- Security.

So now define who, what and where you are in these terms and you should come up with something like this as a Mission Statement.

"We will provide quality fantasy T shirts to Suburbia. We will include fairies, dragons, Goths, monsters and unicorns and have the widest selection we possible can."

Your elevator pitch might be something like this: "We provide quality character based T shirts to children via our office and the internet."

## Tag Line

Now need to be recognised by your customers. Here is where you tag line and logo come into play.

*My tag line - what's that.*

Well if you become as well known as Nike it can be something very short like "Just Do It" - but that is a few years and few £million down the road. Your tag line is a short description of what you do.

Something like "T shirts to sports clubs and schools" which explains what you sell and to whom. It also differentiates you from other companies in your area.

## Logo's

Now you need a logo - it does not need repeating that this should also reflect your brand. If you are saying you are modern and efficient - you don't want an old fashioned, messy looking logo. It should always reflect your brand and be simple and recognisable. You should include it on:

- All your communications.
- Your web site.
- Your products.
- Your packaging.
- Your marketing and promotional materials.
- Your adverts.

## Working with your brand

Your brand is so much more than your logo; it is your company name, your web site and the colours that you use.

Remember your brand allows you to pre-sell your company and products as well as ease the introduction of new products as you become more established. Be consistent with your brand promotion - don't keep changing it as people are more likely to remember things the more they see them. Regular marketing enables you to establish your credibility and relevance to your target market.

## Branding, Packaging And Other Stuff

Everything that your customers and staff see should be "stamped" with your company brand and be instantly recognised as belonging to your company. Let us look at where your will be using your brand. Invoices and order forms should have your company details, contact details and web site as well as your logo.

## Business Name

Pick a great business name that reflects the type of T shirts you are selling and who you are selling to. If you are getting a domain name (and you should, even if you don't want a web site just yet) you need to match this with your company name.

## Packaging

It stands to reason that all your bags and packaging, including that used in delivering your items, should be stamped with your company name, logo, phone number and web site. All packaging should include further Order Forms, and a catalogue.

## Marketing Material

Once again you should market such that your company and how to contact it, is instantly recognisable. How and where you advertise should also back up your brand image. If you are selling family friendly items then you would not advertise in a "lad's mag" for example.

## Starting Small With Your Premises

Sometimes circumstances dictate that you can't afford a retail shop but you really want to get your business started. Many small, retail businesses are not suitable to run from your home base or via a warehouse. Web sites, whilst having low start up costs, also take a lot of marketing and time to become profitable. Why not think about starting a kart or kiosk in a shopping mall? Here are a few points to consider.

## Mall Karts and Kiosks

**As always Location, Location, Location:** The location of your business is crucial to its survival. A store's location can often spell its success or failure. Without sufficient store recognition, a business can suffer poor cash flow and will inevitably fail over time. Your business needs to be physically located out in midst of everyday life, in broad daylight where shoppers can easily find you.

The location itself of the mall plays a huge role in your kart's success. Is the mall located in an isolated part of the city or town, or right in the heart of the action?

You must forecast the level as well as the timing of traffic your business will receive during the morning, midday, and late afternoon on each day of the week. Therefore, you can efficiently establish an employment schedule as well as appropriate operating hours.

Choose your mall carefully so that it has ample traffic of potential customers. Go there with a "clicker" and see how many people pass by per hour. Visit on several different days of the week as well as at different times.

**Quality of Traffic:** It is one thing to have steady traffic, and another to have the kind of traffic that your business needs. Some malls attract low-to-middle income people; others are targeted towards the upper class. Choose wisely.

**Position in the Mall:** Your success in a mall will depend on whether you are located in a section that is conducive to what your business is selling. You should look at the ***complementary nature of the adjacent stores.*** The worst place you could be is by a clothes store that sells T shirts! Look for businesses that are complimentary to what you are selling such as sports stores, gaming stores etc.

You may want to be located near a restaurant where people are already in their "hunger fulfilling" state of mind.

Similarly ***high volume areas*** where lines of patrons form, such as theatres or department stores, are also good mall locations as it could give potential customers several minutes to look in your display or listen to your sales pitch. People will hopefully spend while they wait – if not you have their undivided attention for some time and they will remember you.

**Costs:** Rental costs in shopping malls are often higher than rates in downtown Main Street. You main consideration should be: will the higher traffic compensate for the increased rental cost? If you can easily recover your monthly rental payment and overhead expenses, you're in a good position to make a profit.

**People Buy with their Eyes!** Ensure that you display your products in an tempting manner. Karts, kiosks, stalls and vans and are very good in selling items that are "impulse buys". Make your products appealing and your sales pitch interesting and your sales will increase!

## Market Stalls and Boot Fairs

The same criteria about location appertains to market stalls and boot fairs. Obviously your outlay will be much smaller – but so will your potential income. Care should be taken to ensure that your stall looks professional and well branded otherwise your business will be classed as a "hobby business" and people will expect to pay correspondingly low prices.

## Marketing From Your Retail Site

Whichever low cost option you chose, ensure that you have plenty of brochures available to give out to interested potential customers. Don't leave them on the counter otherwise you will go through a lot of them for little return – save them for the really interested people.  You could leave business cards for anyone to take- people tend to take these only if they are interested.  You should display some good samples as well as a lot of items for sale.  Be prepared to take orders from your stall.

## Marketing Your Business

The first thing you need to do is contact your friends and neighbours and see if they need your services or know someone who does. This usually gets you a few sales to start with. You can consider selling at "mates rates" – discounted rates in order to get yourself some experience and references.

Now set up an advert on your PC. You can print them off, on postcards quite easily. It should read something like this.

---

### Custom T Shirts and Fleeces

We will put your child's or pet's picture on a

T Shirt or Fleece

So that it is totally unique to you.

From £10 and we take the photo!

For more details,

Call Company X: 123-4567 - ABC T Shirts

---

If you don't feel that you can do this yourself. Then go to Vistaprint, Lulu etc. who will print some off for you at not too high a price.

You can also put a similar advert in your local papers if that is affordable.

In essence, you now have a professional advertising "billboard" and it is time to use a bit of shoe leather. Put the leaflets on notice boards in supermarkets, shops, clubs, offices etc. Always ask first.

If you want to sell to clubs, societies, hotels etc then now is the time to "dial and smile". You need to get contact details from the yellow pages, internet or your contacts. Call them up or send them your information pack, with the aim of obtaining an appointment to discuss your services. The next chapter explains what to do on this appointment.

If you also decided to use business cards – use the front to put your company name, contact details and a one line description of your services. Start to leave these wherever you are allowed to - anywhere busy people and new parents or pet owners can be found.

A good supply of business cards for your staff as well, in order to advertise your services to others they come in contact with.

A great idea would be to have magnetic signs made for your company and services. Place these signs on the sides of the cars your people use for transportation to each job, and later on, to the sides of your company van or car.

One other form of advertising you should go with would be a display ad in the yellow pages of your telephone directory.

Look at getting yourself a stall at the local market, the car boot sale, a kiosk in the mall etc. which will get you a lot of exposure and hopefully some sales for little outlay. We go into this later in the book.

It takes a short while to start up any kind of company. Start touting for small contracts to begin with particularly those that you can do yourself.

## Interacting With Your Customers

Once you spread the word that you're in the business of T shirt printing you'll have no trouble at all keeping busy!

When prospective clients call or email you, explain your services and prices. When selling large or bespoke orders it is best to either ask for a 50% deposit or a 100% payment. This is because once you have finished the service; it is sometimes hard to obtain the payment due. Make sure that you receive all the payment due before you finish the service.

## First Contact

When a prospective customer calls or your telephone sales pitch is positive, have your appointment book and a pen handy. Be friendly and enthusiastic. Explain what you do and offer to show a few samples.

When they ask how much you charge, simply give them a wide range and say that you will give a firm cost quote, once you've discussed their requirements. Then without much of a pause, ask if 4:30 this afternoon would be convenient for them, or if 5:30 would be better.

You must pointedly ask if they can come to make your cost proposal at a certain time, or the decision may be put off, and you may come up with a "no sale." You may prefer to invite them to visit you if you have a suitable reception area.

Just as soon as you have an agreement on the time and place to make you cost proposal and marked it in your appointment book, ask for their name, address and telephone number.

Jot this information down on a 3 by 5 card, along with the date and the notation: Prospective Customer. Then you file this card in a permanent card file.

Save these cards, because there are literally hundreds of ways to turn this prospect file into real cash, once you've accumulated a sizeable number of names, addresses and phone numbers. If you have a suitable computer program, then enter the details there as well.

## Estimating

When you go to see your prospect in person, always be on time. A couple of minutes early won't hurt you, but a few minutes late will definitely be detrimental to your closing the sale. If they are coming to you then ensure that you give good directions and are ready for them.

Always be well groomed. Dress as a successful business owner. Be confident and sure of yourself; be knowledgeable about what you can do as well as understanding of the prospect's needs and wants. Do not smoke, even if invited by the prospect. It's important to appear methodical, thorough and professional

A little small talk after the sale is appropriate, but becoming too friendly is not. You create an impression, and preserve it, by maintaining a business-like relation ship.

When you go to make your cost estimate, take along a ruled tablet on a clipboard a calculator, your appointment book and your sample designs.

You should also have at least two of your sales packs (one for the customer and the other for her friend that may also need your services) and a blank contract (more of this later). A receipt book would also be a good idea. You can buy folios in stationary stores that will keep these all tidy.

If they choose one of your sample designs, fine, but if they want a particular design of their own, now is the time to ask for photos or start jotting down all their requirements, including sizes and colours.

You should hopefully come up with a drawing of what they require in front of them. Get them to sign off these details and picture so that there is no dispute later. You will probably have to come back to them with a firm price. Make sure that it is possible for you to actually produce the T shirts!

Discuss when they need the T shirts and if you are delivering them or if they are collecting from you.

Now complete the contract for them, summarising what you have just agreed and confirm that you will send her a typed up list of all the T shirt customisation details you have just completed. Ask them for confirmation on the contract and for a deposit if applicable. Also offer them a sales pack for their friend who may need your services.

## The Art of Selling

It has been said that a sale is really closed long before the seller makes the final pitch to the customer. In many ways, this is very true. Many customers make a decision to buy in five minutes or less of being introduced to the product. As a successful entrepreneur, it is up to you to make those five minutes really count.

There are a couple of important things that take place in this five minute window of opportunity.

First, the customer decides whether or not it is worth the time to learn more about the product. If the answer is no, then even thirty minutes of a great pitch will accomplish nothing.

Second, the customer will think of major obstacles that will prevent the purchase from taking place. If a customer decides the product is out of reach for some reason, that will make everything that follows that first five minutes of no value whatsoever.

Your job is to overcome both these issues and encourage the prospect to not only desire the product, but also be able to visualise actively using the product to great advantage. Here are a few ideas on how to accomplish this:

- **Ascertain the needs of your client.** This means asking clarifying questions that help to narrow the focus of the presentation to what is important to the customer. For example, if a primary need of the client is to pay the phone bill at the end of the month, tailor the presentation to show how the product can directly help achieve that goal.

- **Be prepared to address common obstacles.** Many obstacles are not unique – people from all sorts of background will share the same concerns. Proactively bring those up during those first five minutes and quickly demonstrate how they are non-issues. This will make it possible to dispose of those concerns and hold the attention and interest of the prospect past that five minute window.

- **Always close with benefits**. Some of those benefits may have to do with overcoming obstacles, but go a little further than that. Using the phone bill example again, point out how the product can make it easier every month to pay the bill – not just the one that is due the end of this month.

Making the most of those first five minutes will greatly increase your chances of closing the sale. Spend some time working on a model presentation and critique the results. This will help you move with greater prowess when the real deal comes along. Congratulations you have just made a sale!

## Promotional Mugs

Promotional mugs would be a great and useful way to advertise your service and reach new people in the community and potential customers or even potential future business associates.

It's an affordable thing to do, especially if you can print the mugs yourself. Some research will find the best place to buy bulk mugs. Another option is to locate a business that will copy your logo to the mug for you if you do not have the time or experience to do it yourself.

You need to create an eye catching logo and phrase that fully states what you do, i.e., T shirt printing, and be sure to put your website or a number where they can reach you. There's nothing more frustrating than seeing something you are interested in and having no clue where to go to find out about it.

Now you want to make a list of how to go about getting them out. Put a pile of business cards in them and drop them off at local businesses. Leave some in your front office or on your market staff for people to pick up?

Promotional mugs are just a start to promoting your business further. When people see or hear your ad many times yet don't contact you that doesn't mean they will forget about you.

When and if something happens where they need your services, they will remember your ad and automatically want to try you out. It never hurts to overdo it sometimes because that will get you noticed and help you continue to grow in your business.

Give promotional mugs a try, if all else fails and it doesn't turn out like you wanted remember what you learned in the process and how much that will benefit you.

## T Shirt Printing As A Promotional Product

Many people do not realise the value and importance that T shirt printing can provide. T shirt printing is very popular and useful for many reasons and offers different benefits for different people which depend upon what you are using the shirt printing for.

One major benefit that T shirt printing offers is advertisement and promotion. Advertising and promotion is done every day with shirt printing and is vital to the existence of not only companies, but also to the promotion of certain products. Whether it is a movie, cartoon character, or even a local business, T shirt printing provides great advertising. In fact, many companies create a product and not only use shirt printing to advertise their product, but also make money from selling the shirts.

Many businesses also use shirt T printing to give away free shirts with their logo or company information on it to obtain advertising from people wearing the free shirts. Without T shirt printing this would not be possible and they would also lose out on the millions of dollars that T shirt printing provides for them.

Another benefit that T shirt printing provides is letting us be able to express ourselves creatively. With computer and printing technology advanced as it is, people everywhere are now able to have their own creations on their shirts.

They can use personal photos, create their own images, and make anything they want. For this reason, T shirt printing has become an outlet for people to express themselves without any restriction through their own designs. Many shirts used in T shirt printing can reflect personal things about people as well as show you a person's personality.

## Other Stuff Your Can Sell

As well as T-shirts, polo shirts and fleeces you can also easily add the following items:

- Mouse pads
- Tote Bags
- Puzzles
- Coffee cup wrappers
- Place Mats
- Aprons
- Baby Bibs
- Pillow Cases
- Flags
- and many other fabric items

With extra machinery you can also add ceramic mugs and caps.

If you invest in a more powerful sublimation printer you can also print onto more sturdy items such as:

- License plate holders
- Vehicle magnetic signs
- Shop signs
- Key Chains
- Luggage Tags
- Clocks
- Ceramic Tiles
- Plaques
- Clip Boards
- Serving Trays
- Picture Frames Etc.

## Buying And Selling Wholesale

Clubs, churches, school, teams and many other groups buy custom printed shirts for their organisations. They usually do this through wholesale because it is considerably cheaper that way. This is a great market for you to get into and you should spend some of your marketing time in chasing this work. Of course your prices will be lower for a large order, but you will save time in setting up the designs.

In order to meet these needs, or as you get bigger you will need to buy wholesale. To most people, the word wholesale equates to being inexpensive. The larger quantity of items you need, the lower the price goes. Before buying anything wholesale you want to check out the prices of everyone that offers that option. The brand of the shirt does not always mean you will get a great quality tee shirt. Do not be fooled into thinking the more expensive tee shirts have better quality outcome.

Some places go by size as well. If you are buying for youth, they will be cheaper. Just keep in mind all the different aspects of wholesale buying before actually buying something.

## Administration

Administration is very important. Without good administration your company will quickly disintegrate into chaos and you won't know who has what and who needs to pay for services and who needs them to be cleaned and when. Your administration should include ways of controlling or managing the following:

- Collecting money from your customers
- Banking money.
- Managing enquiries and complaints.
- Invoice and bill payment.
- Accounts and book keeping including, payroll, banking, taxes and VAT/taxes.
- Purchasing and auditing equipment. At least once a year and preferably quarterly, equipment must be checked against your accounts and for the need to be repaired.
- Salary and commission payments.
- Staff training and development.

It may seem a lot, but if you start small and get yourself a good accounts package, a good accountant and bank manager it is a lot easier.

## Customer Administration

- Set up a file for each of your customers with their contact details, what you have agreed to do, the price to be charged and any other details. Keep a folder/file for each customer. Add each order to the file – latest order on top. The file should include all contact details. If you have a number of orders per client put a list of orders on top and tick them off as you complete them. If you have a lot of customers have a customer number format.

- You should also keep a record of money due and paid. You should be able to find a good accounting system very easily. Always give a receipt and chase overdue accounts.

- Make a To-Do list of all your orders and tick off those that have been completed. Put in order of importance/when delivered.

- Keep a detailed diary of when they have to be delivered by. In the diary also note what extra services were requested and what payment you need for the service.

### Writing A Winning Proposal?

You've been working with a potential client and you think that you finally have the future project all worked out – then they ask you for a proposal. You've seen this great potential project but you need to bid for it. So how do you write that proposal that is going to win you the business?

Well first of all let's look at what the proposal should do. Win of course, but before that you have to:

- Make your company stand out from the others as well as reflect the values and brand of your company.
- Offer the solution that is required in a format that is easily understood.
- Be well priced so as to attract the client, provide a profit for your company as well as opportunities for you both to work together in the future.
- Be well structured, well written and well presented.

Bearing in mind the above, your proposal should look something like this:

1) Thanks for the opportunity.

2) Your understanding of the job that needs to be done.

3) How you would complete the job, how long it will take and who will do it.

4) Why your company is the best for the job.

5) Your price – with subject breakdowns if appropriate.

6) Any "must haves" assumptions made etc in getting to the price.

7) Last thanks and way forward.

Item 5 and 6 should be on their own page so that they can be removed if necessary.

Remember to put your company details and contact details on the header of each page and your copyrights, date and page number of number of pages on each footer.

When you send off the proposal, on time of course, include a brief cover letter, with:

- Your contact details.
- The name of the person who is their contact for this bid.
- Your thanks for the opportunity.
- A very brief overview of bid - no price.
- A time frame that bid is current.
- Your thanks and hope to hear from them soon.

Now sit back and pride yourself on a job well done. Good luck

## Putting Your Business On The Internet

J ust about anyone can put a web site up on the internet and now days it is quite easy. You have two choices as how to set up your website:

- As a shop window for your company, with contact details etc.
- As a fully working site with ecommerce facilities.

Which ever option you choose, you first need a god domain name. Go to a good domain provider like enom, godaddy, namecheap NOT registerfly and spend under £10 on a domain. Choose a domain name that has the word T shirt and or printing in it. This will help with your search engine positioning as well as act as a memory jog to your potential customers.

## As A Shop Window

Hop over to hostgator or similar and then buy a monthly hosting account. With that will come a site maker - where you can easily set up a web site using one of thousands of templates. You can add payment processor linkages, forums etc.

The only problem you will have is you want to sell promote or talk about illegal activities, terrorist activities or sex! Also if you want a high usage activity such as MySpace etc.

## As A Full Site

You will probably need to get this especially written and designed for you. Put your project on sites like guru/elance/scriptlance etc and find a competitive quote.

Get yourself a PayPal account or similar so that you can take payment on your web site. This is much more secure and quicker than taking checks.

## Factors To Remember

Always consider your target market when designing your web site. Include some helpful information about your subject matter but nothing that will give away what you are trying to sell! Ensure that your contact details can be freely found and that details of your company and services are clearly set out.

As you will be asking for money before you deliver something – make your potential customer feel comfortable making payment and tell them what will happen next.

Respond to all enquiries and purchases very quickly. If this is difficult then set up an autoresponder to confirm you have received their enquiry/payment and will get back to them within a few hours. Place references that you have received from past

## An Internet Marketing Strategy

Ok, you've got your web site set up, you are sure that it is search engine friendly and you are pretty certain what your customers want. You've identified at least 3 products that you want to promote and you think that they meet your potential customer's needs. So now what?

Well unfortunately the days, that I can remember, of "build it and they will come" have long gone. Unless you promote your web site – no one will know that you are there and no visitors means no sales. So where so you go from here?

Well take a deep breath, a pen and paper and let's start on your Marketing Strategy. Briefly for a new business, with a relatively inexperienced marketer, your strategy will probably include the following options:

- Pay Per Click Advertising
- Article Marketing
- Email Marketing
- Community Marketing
- Classified Advertising

Let's get started – and before you start panicking, you are just writing your Marketing Strategy. This course will explain how to do all of the following.

## Your Advertising Kit

For each of your programs/products

1. Write a short advert – say 50 words.
2. Write a very short advert – say 15 words
3. Write a short article – say about 400 – 600 words.
4. Decide on your keywords – say about 30 – 50 words.

## Your Marketing Kit

For your web site theme

1. Write at least 6 short auto responder messages.
2. Find or write at least 2 giveaway products.

## Your Marketing Tools

1. Your web site
2. An autoresponder
3. A good email account

Put all of these together into your first Marketing Strategy.

1. **Submit your web site to all the major search engines.** This will start to get your web site noticed. As this takes a long time, it needs to be the first thing that you do. You can do this yourself or pay someone else to do this for you. We provide this service for our customers for £20 a month, which includes submission to Google, Yahoo and MSN.

2. **Set up your autoresponder form** on your web site and load your messages into the autoresponder. Ensure that you offer one of the giveaway products as a bonus for signing onto your ezine. The second giveaway can be set up for message 3 or 4. Your messages should be sent in the following intervals. Day 1,3,7,7,7,7

3. **Set up your download pages**, for your bonus products as well as the products you are selling. Ensure that you provide an extra offer on each download page.

4. **Submit your article** – including your resource box, to about 6 major ezine article sites. Limit yourself to 6 at the moment. Each of these submissions, if accepted will give you a link to your web site. If too many links to your new web site appear very quickly, search engines assume that you have been using "black hat" SEO tactics (a total no no) and will not list your site.

5. **Identify 4 forums** that discuss the topics of your web site. Set yourself up an account name that describes you well. We use the name "Biz Guru" which is our trade mark and name. Set up your signature to include your web site address. You now have 4 good links to your web site.

6. **Answer Questions:** Start answering questions asked within the forums. Do NOT post adverts for your web site or products. Use this time to establish your credentials. If you answer questions well and contribute to the forums, your web site tag will be noticed.

7. **Set up a PPC campaign** – you can start with the smaller search engines first. Take your very small advert and your keywords and use them in your campaign. Most search engines will help you with your choice of keywords. Remember to set a budget and test, test and test again until you get quality and converting traffic.

8. **Set up some classified ads**. You can do this one of two ways: i) choose one or two major sites/email lists and advertise with them. ii) use an ezine ad blaster to send your ad out to numerous low quality places.

9. **Test, Update and Modify**. Review, change and add to your PPC keywords. Submit more articles and adverts. Start tactfully promoting your products in the forums.

Your challenge will be to be listed in the major search engines and then get traffic. Now market your web site like mad. It will take several months to make an impact in the major search engines. So build up your local custom whilst you are doing this. www.GetIntoGoogleFast.com – Does exactly what is says in the domain!

## Staff

Expansion means growth, involving people working for you, more jobs to sell, and greater profits. Don't let it frighten you, for you have gained experience by starting gradually. After all - your aim in starting a business of your own was to make money, wasn't it? And expanding means more helpers so you don't have to work your self to death!

So, just as soon as you possibly can, recruit and hire other people to do the work for you. The first people you hire should be people to handle customer sales.

You can obtain good staff by word of mouth, advertising in your local Job Centre, supermarket etc. Look in your local university and local school and ask amongst friends. You will find a lot of people who want to work part time here - as well as those that are able to work early in the morning or in the evening if you need them.

You can start these people at minimum wage or a bit above, and train them to complete every job assignment in a set timeframe. You might consider hiring people on a contract basis so that if they don't work you don't pay. You don't get loyalty here though.

You should also outfit them in a kind of uniform with your company name on the back of their T shirts.

## Customer Contracts

When you're dealing with customers, sometimes things can go wrong. It might be your fault, it might be their fault or it might be no-one's fault -- but if you didn't make a contract, then you'll all suffer.

## Why Do I Need Contracts?

A contract gives you a sound legal base for your business, and some guarantee that you're going to get paid for your work without you having to ask the customer for payment in advance. In the event of a dispute, the contract lays down what the agreement was so that you can point to it and say what was agreed. If you ever end up having to go to court (let's hope you won't), the contract is what the judge's decision will be based on.

Without a contract, you leave yourself vulnerable and open to exploitation. Someone could claim that the terms they agreed with you were different to what you say they were or that they never signed up for anything at all and so they won't pay.

It's especially common to see big businesses mistreat small ones, thinking that they won't have the knowledge or the money to do anything about it. Essentially, contracts take away your customers' ability to hold non-payment over your head, and give you the ability to hold it over theirs instead.

## Written and Verbal Contracts

It is important to point out the distinction in the law between a verbal (spoken) contract and a proper, written one. A verbal contract is binding in theory, but in practice can be very hard to prove. A written contract, on the other hand, is rock-solid proof of what you're saying.

You might think that you're never going to get into a dispute with your customers, but it's all too common to find yourself in a little disagreement.

They will often want to get you to do some 'small' amount of extra work to finish the job or make it better; not realising that doing so would completely obliterate your profit margin.

For this reason, you should be very wary of doing anything with nothing but a verbal contract. On the other hand, if you were incautious or too trusting and only got a verbal contract, it could still go some way towards helping you, especially if there were witnesses.

## Won't It Be Expensive?

Written contracts don't necessarily need to be formal contracts, which are drawn up by a lawyer with 'contract' written at the top and signed by both parties.

These kinds of contracts are the most effective, but can be expensive to have produced, not to mention intimidating to customers.

The most common kind of written contract, oddly enough, is a simple letter. If you send a customer a letter laying out your agreement before you start work, and they write back to agree to it, that is enough to qualify as a written contract, with most of the protections it affords. It is best to get confirmation from your customer that they have received this contract.

If you are doing high-value work for some clients, though, it could be worth the time and trouble of having your lawyer write a formal contract, or at least of doing it yourself and getting a lawyer to look it over.

Formal contracts will give you more protection if the worst happens, and there's nothing to stop you from making it a one-off expense only by re-using the same contract for multiple customers. **PLEASE: TAKE PROFESSIOANAL ADVICE.**

## Contracts for Small Purchases.

Obviously it would be silly to expect everyone who buys some £10 product or service from you to sign a contract, or write back indicating their agreement to your terms. In this situation, you should have a statement of the 'terms and conditions' that your customer is agreeing to by buying from you, and they should have to tick some kind of box indicating their agreement before you send anything.

## The Top 5 First-Year Mistakes

Even once you've got past the starting-up stage, there are still plenty mistakes to be made, and most of them are going to be made in your make-or-break year -- the first one. Here are the top five things to avoid.

## Waiting for Customers to Come to You

Too many people wait for their customers to phone, or come to the door, or whatever. They get one or two customers through luck, but nothing like enough to even begin paying their costs. These people sit around, looking at their competitors doing lots of business, and wonder what they're doing wrong.

You can't be like this. You have to go out there and actively try to find customers. Talk to people, call them, meet with them -- whatever you do, don't just sit there!

## Spending Too Much on Advertising

So everyone tells you that the only way to get ahead in business is to advertise. Well, that's true, but you need to make sure that you stick to inexpensive advertising methods when you're starting out. Spending hundreds of dollars for an ad in the local newspaper might turn out to get you very few new customers, and you will have spent your entire advertising budget on it.

Make your money go further with leaflets, direct mail or email -- these are easily targetable campaign methods with high response rates and low costs. Remember that it is always better to spend money on an offer than on an ad, and always better to spend money on an ad than on a delivery method.

## Being Too Nice

When you're running your own business, it can be tempting to be everyone's friend, giving discounts at the drop of a hat and making sure that you don't hassle or inconvenience anyone.

That's all well and good, until you find that your Good Samaritan act has just halved your profit margin without lowering the cost to the customer by very much at all.

Sometimes, you need to realise that you've got to be harsh to make a profit. Give people discounts to encourage them to buy or to come back, not because you like them or feel sorry for them. Don't be afraid to be ruthless in your pursuit of business success. Nice guys don't finish last, but they are running in a different race -- one with much less prize money. If that doesn't bother you, of course, then feel free to go for it.

## Not Using the Phone

You'd be surprised just how common phone fears are -- if you're scared of the phone, you're not alone by any means. Many people are terrified of making phone calls, and avoid them wherever possible. I have seen more than one business owner reduced to tears on the phone and trying desperately to hide it from the customer.

You need to try your best to overcome your fears, as talking to customers on the phone is almost as good as meeting them for real. Letters and emails are useless by comparison. The best way to overcome phone fears varies from person to person, but it can often be as simple as making the phone fun, by calling friends and relatives often for a while and getting used to it. Alternatively, try working in telemarketing for a while -- if that doesn't make normal phone use look like a walk in the park by comparison, then nothing will.

## Hiring Professionals for Everything

It can be tempting to think that, since you're starting out, you should just find a company or person to do every little thing you need. People seem to especially overspend on design services.

You might think it'd be great to have fancy graphics all over your website, but would it really increase sales? If I saw it, it would put me right off. Likewise, a slick brochure often fails to say anything more than 'I'm going to charge you a premium to pay for my expensive brochures'.

Don't hire someone unless you can demonstrate that the service they're going to provide will increase your profits by more than the amount you're spending -- if you're not sure, try it yourself first, and you can always upgrade it later.

### Problems You May Have

As in any business you will get problems, sometimes just knowing what you may face is a great help.

- Some customers use office email to correspond with you. Make sure that you are discrete with the headings used on the emails to them.

- Some customers are never satisfied. Just make any reasonable changes that are requested. Similarly some have a very high opinion of their very basic experience. Be polite and patient.

- Some customers may have problems explaining what they want – this is where your product sheet comes in handy. Make sure that you write down everything that they request and get this agreed to.

- Some customers are very slow in replying – ensure that you give them a time limit to reply and then send two further reminders – telling them when the last one is.

## Time for a Holiday: But How?

When you've been working long and hard at your business for a while, you might feel like you've earned yourself a little break. There are business owners out there who haven't taken a real holiday since they started their business -- including some who started their business as long as five years ago!

After all, how can you ever just desert your business and your customers and go bronze yourself on the beach? How can you avoid being on call 24/7 throughout your holiday? Well, everyone deserves some time to themselves at least once a year, if they want to keep being productive and avoid stress. Here's what to do.

## Tell People When You Are Going Away.

You can't just disappear when you're running a business -- you need to let people know long in advance that you're not going to be available, and make sure that they have everything they need to manage without you while you're away.

It's best to schedule your holiday not to interfere too much with the business.

However much you might want to have your holiday in the summer, it's important to remember that every business has its quiet months, and you should schedule your holiday in the period where they seem to be.

## Change Your Voicemail Message.

A quick and simple way to let people know that you've gone away is to change your voicemail message. This allows you to still hear what people have to say when you get back, and stops them from wondering why you never seem to answer your phone.

A good format for the message is as follows: 'Hi, this is [your name] at [company name]. I'm sorry I'm not in the office right now, but I will be back on [give a date]. If you leave a message, I will be sure to get back to you'.

If you work from home don't give a coming back date unless you want to invite the local thief into your home!

## Set Up an Email Auto responder.

Similar to a voicemail message, but less commonly used, is the email auto responder. Again, you don't want people to wonder why their emails are going unanswered, so your best bet is to set up your email program to automatically reply to any email you get with a message saying that you've gone away.

Example: 'Hello, and thank you for your email. This is an auto responder, as I'm away on holiday until [date]. I have received your email, however, and will respond to it upon my return. I apologies for any inconvenience to you, and I am willing to make an offer of 10% off your next order to make it up to you.' The special offer for people who get the auto responder is a nice touch -- it makes them feel lucky that they emailed you while you were away, instead of frustrated.

## Don't Stay Away Too Long.

Of course, when you go on holiday, you're relying on people being willing to wait for you. That means you can't really take the kids to Disney World for two weeks, or spend a month staying with a friend abroad -- it's just too long to be away from your business for.

You should regard a weekend away as ideal (it avoids the whole problem for the most part), and a week as the maximum you can allow yourself. Don't let people make you feel bad about only taking one-week holidays: after all, you could always have more than one each year.

## Alternatively: Get Someone to Look after the Business.

If you really want to get away for longer, or it's essential that your customers don't have any break in service, then you could consider getting someone to look after your business.

This could be an existing member of staff that you make your 'deputy', to be in charge while you're away, or it could be someone who's related to you and has some experience running a business. You could even hand the business over to a competitor that you're friendly with and share the profits with them, if you think they're trustworthy and they could handle it.

Enjoy your holiday!

## In Conclusion

One of the most important aspects of this business is asking for, and allowing your customers to refer other prospects to you. All of this happens, of course, as a result of your giving fast, dependable service. You might even set up a promotional notice on the back of your business card (to be left at each job is completed) offering £2 off their T shirt when they refer you to a new prospect.

This is definitely a high profit business, requiring only an investment of time and organisation on your part to get started. With a low investment, little or no over head requirement, this is an ideal business opportunity with a growth curve that accelerates at an unprecedented rate.

---

**Brought to You By The Biz Guru**
*"If you need help with your business – click or brick – we're here to help"*
**www.StartMyNewBusiness.com**

---

# Profitable New T Shirt Printing Business

## Index:

# Profitable New T Shirt Printing Business

Lightning Source UK Ltd.
Milton Keynes UK
UKOW05f2159271113

221973UK00001B/193/P